Nobody told me…

K V

BookLeaf Publishing

India | USA | UK

Presentation by *BookLeaf Publishing*

Web: www.bookleafpub.com

E-mail: info@bookleafpub.com

ISBN: 978-93-5744-998-4

First edition 2022

DEDICATION

To Maxwell Alric,

Thank you for bringing this new light to my life and walking with me through the darkness. You are the reason my heart beats.

Love Mummy

ACKNOWLEDGEMENT

Without the support of the community mental health team and everyone they referred me to, I wouldn't have survived. Thank you for fighting for me when I didn't want to.

PREFACE

These are a series of poems that explore the depression I felt after giving birth to my son. It was hard to verbalise the mess in my head but writing made it easier.

Nobody told me…

Nobody told me what motherhood would be
like.
That it would break me, make me, shake me and
forsake me.
Nobody told me I would love him with my
whole being, to the point I had no love left for
myself.
Nobody told me all the things I would miss;
My body, my bed, my freedom, my sleep, my
independence, myself.
Nobody told me all the things I would gain;
Two little eyes that hold the world, a million
smiles, a laugh that feels like sunshine.
Nobody told me how much I would cry, how
often I would want to die.
Nobody told me that my little boy would be the
reason I hang on but also the reason I want to let
go.
Nobody told me I would feel alone.
Nobody told me my house wouldn't feel like my
home.
Nobody told me nothing would ever be the
same.

Nobody told me...

I don't remember asking…

Once you have a baby
Everyone thinks they have a say
They needlessly tell you what to do
How they think you should spend your day
There's just no need to tell me
I've never asked for your advice
But I can't tell you just to shove it
Society tells me that isn't nice
But this is all new to me
And I deserve a chance
To figure out the kind of mother I want to be
Without being shunned in advance
I wish that people understood
The kind of change that you endure
When everything you have ever known
Suddenly becomes unsure
We should be given space and time
To figure it all out
If I wanted your advice
I would ask…

What is wrong with me?

I look around
And I can't help but compare
There must be something I'm missing
Something just isn't there
They all look so happy
Like becoming a mum has given them new life
Now don't get me wrong,
I love you
My feelings are strong
But having you has felt like the end of my life
I question our connections
There are days I just can't
I don't want to hold you
I can't stand your gaze
It wasn't like this at the start
I used to want to hold you,
Every minute of the day
Now sometimes, I wish you would just go away
It makes me wonder what
Has gone wrong inside my brain
All these other mothers must never have these
thoughts

Maybe I'm insane
I wish that I was better
That's what you deserve
That's what everyone wants to see
One of these picture perfect mothers
Instead of me

Down the rabbit hole

Some days I feel like Alice
Nothing is what it seems
The walls and doors all shrink and close
And I am stuck somewhere In between
I can't find the way out
And I'm sure I'm always late
The rooms all spin,
The cues all change
You are different everyday
And nothing is ever the same
As soon as I have something figured out,
We hit another turn
I don't feel like I'm ever winning
Why is it all so hard to learn?
I don't know how much longer I can do this,
Everyday is an uphill fight
The days are long and I'm all wrong
But most of all I dread the nights.
The house feels so empty,
The halls are so dark.
There's no company, just you and me,
And the screaming of your song.

Will I ever find the way out?
The exit to the light?
I'm spiralling now,
Falling down, down, down
And whenever I think I've reached the bottom,
I find out there's further to fall

Here at the bottom of this rabbit hole,
I can't see the way out
And I've accepted that this is my life now,
This pain, this loneliness, this life has become
my tomb.
And I'm sorry that I wasn't strong enough to
carry you till you were old enough to walk
But I've been falling since you entered this
world and now I am truly lost.

Today I can

Today I can love you,
Hold you and smile.
Today I don't feel so heavy
Today doesn't scare me like yesterday did
Today I can do this
Today I can be your mum
Today I can
It's all the tomorrows that still worry me

You need me…

Im cold but you need me
Im tired but you need me
Im sick but you need me
Im sad but you need me
Im bleeding but you need me
Im dying but you need me
I need space but you need me
I need me… but you need me more

I'm not strong enough…

My body can't take the weight
My mind can't take the thoughts
My heart can't take the guilt
How can I feel anything but love for him?
Why am I feeling so miserable?
Why am I angry?

I have no control.
Not over my body
My mind
My thoughts
My sleep
My time
My life

I know I love him
Yes, that's what I know
But some days I don't feel it
I can't feel it
Some days I just can't be his mum
I don't want him to touch me
Or look at me

It's not fair on him
But some days my demons are driving
And I'm not even trying to swim
I'm just trying not to drown

Clinging to the ledge

I've been having a hard time
Accepting what they say
This will pass
You're not a bad mum
That's how depression gets its way
But up until yesterday
They have all been speaking from the outside
They didn't know what it's like
To look at your child and feel nothing
They don't know what it's like to see a smiling
baby
And want to die
I took great comfort in speaking to someone
who had been there
Not the same journey, but the same darkness
To see someone who had managed to pull
them-self up from the ledge and now reaches out
a hand
Just knowing someone who had been there,
I started to believe that maybe I would get
through this
Maybe it would end

With a lifetime with my baby
Instead of with me dead

It's all Noise

Trying to explain this noise in my head
All these thoughts that I'm having
Why I wish I was dead
They just don't understand it
But honestly how could they?
If you've never been there,
With a blade to your wrist,
How could you understand this dark wish?
The desire to die
But also to live
Just a little cut here
It's easy to forgive
It's better than the alternative
The solution that the noise suggests
Cut deeper and deeper
Till there's nothing left.
I know you are just trying to help
Asking me to try a different way
But by the time I get to that point,
I don't have a say.
It's either release it all now
Or surrender for good
I'm just doing all that I can
To survive another day
For my little man.

Living in the grey

Am I feeling good or am I feeling numb?
I honestly can't tell
What has my life become?
I don't feel like crying
But sometimes I still think about dying
I still want to quit
I'm still over it
But it's different than before
It's not quite so frantic
I can calm myself down
Maybe I can handle it
But then something minor happens
Something that shouldn't matter so much
And it all becomes too tough
And I feel myself shift
Falling back down that rift
But I still haven't hit the bottom.
Just a free fall
Nothing I do matters at all
What's the point of trying again?
When it's just wasting time
Waiting for the end…

Why am I the default?

Who decided that I would be the default?
You are his parent too
I didn't make him by myself
I shouldn't be the glue
Holding this family together
When you're trying to pull it apart
It's time to grow up and show yourself
Show me what's inside your heart.
If I'm doing this alone,
Then why am I still here?
Do I stay out of love?
Do I stay out of fear?
I can see that you love him,
But you didn't lose anything when he was born
You didn't have to surrender your time, body or life
And the worst part is you left me alone.

So now it's time to pick
Because I will not wait around
Are you a default parent too
Or are you an error?

Not to be found.

Failure as a Mother

Why is it that the further I get away from you,
the closer I get to me?
Going back to work is the happiest I have ever
been
I feel so alive and so much like me
But then I feel guilty.
Why wasn't I better?
Why wasn't I happy spending time with you?
What am I doing wrong?
Everyone tells me you are such a chill baby
But I couldn't handle you
I couldn't handle me
I needed that stability
That space.
I needed something I was good at
I needed that piece of my old life
I feel like such a failure
I wanted you so badly
I love you with everything I am
But it wasn't enough
To keep me alive
I needed a piece of me
So I could stick around for you
But ultimately it made me a failure
And I hate myself for it.

Caught in a loop

Sometimes I'm fine
Sometimes I'm good and
Sometimes I'm crying
Just because I could.
Nothing has triggered it
It's because I finally stopped.
I stopped running from my thoughts
They have me trapped again
I can't escape
There's no way out
I let them suffocate me.
I don't want to feel this way
But how do I make them stop?
They are telling me how to change
Things that are in the past
I know I can't go back
So why does my mind torture me?

Today is a good day

Today is a good day
One of the few I've had
I feel so connected with you
I wanna smile and dance
You laugh when I laugh
You smile at me
Is this what motherhood is meant to be?
I don't want this feeling to end
Everything just feels right
I know it won't last for me
It never does
But today, just for today
I feel like I am full of love
I have no thoughts of death
No tears in my eyes,
I just want to hold you close
Feel your warmth
And live the best day of our lives.

The sky is falling

I feel like the sky is falling
I know it's not
I can see that it's not
Everyone else is going on with life like it's not
But I can feel it crashing down upon me.
I don't know how to stop these feelings,
How to reason with myself
There's no in between,
I'm either fine or broken.
These are the thoughts I left unspoken.
I don't need people to know how crazy I am
I never used to be this way, but giving birth
changed me
Brought all my insecurities and trauma to the
surface.
Remade me into a mess of a human who
constantly feels like she is not enough to do this
I'm not enough to be your mum
I'm not enough to see the sun
I'm not enough to keep this life
I'm not enough to continue this fight
I can feel the sky falling,
This weight upon my chest
But on those good days, I can look at you and
Forget about the rest.

Closing doors

It's feels like I'm locked in a room, the door is
shut and I'm stuck here,
I'm trapped in this version of my life and
nothing is the same
But you just get to visit,
Wander in and out as you please
That doesn't seem fair
He's your son too
Why am I the full time parent
But you are optional?
I don't like feeling trapped
It makes me wanna run away
But then I have a panic attack
About who would be here to stay.
To take care of my littlest love
To show him right from wrong.
He is the reason I am still alive.
He is the reason I am not gone.
But you, you are the reason I am losing control
Every time I feel good about myself, you shut
another door
You know exactly how to hurt me
Exactly what to say
All because you get to choose when to parent
But I don't.

I never get to switch off
If I try to do something for myself
You carry on and say it's too much.
Part of me wants to end it all
Just so you have to step up
But that's not fair on our baby
He doesn't deserve to have to grow up before his
time.
So I will stay
I will stay for him
But this life between us is growing thin.

So much guilt

There's so much guilt
There so much pain
Memories of your first smile
Clouded by rain
How will I ever get past
All the sadness I feel?
I wasted our time together
Wishing you weren't real.
Now I'm excited to spend time with you
It's been eight months
What's wrong with me?
Why didn't I feel this way earlier?
Surely you must hate me?
Will you feel resentful because I was a mess?
Did I break you?
Did I show you enough love?
Will I ever get past this guilt?

I love you more

In spite of everything,
I love you more
More than the tears
The fears
The sleepless night
All the fights.
I love you more than the things I've lost
Everything it cost.
More than the body that is no longer mine.
More than the life I left behind.
More than the guilt I feel.
More than everything that is real.
I love you more than life itself
I love you, my baby boy.
Even though it took me so long to feel this bond,
I love you.

www.ingramcontent.com/pod-product-compliance
Lightning Source LLC
LaVergne TN
LVHW021342200726

843509LV00014B/2629